GEOGRAPHY FOR THE LOST

Kapka Kassabova is a cross-genre writer with a special interest in deep journeying, exploring human geographies, and the hidden narratives of places, people, and peripheries. She has published two poetry collections with Bloodaxe, *Someone else's life* (2003) and *Geography for the Lost* (2007). Born in 1973 in Sofia, Bulgaria, she emigrated to New Zealand with her family in 1992, where published two poetry collections, *All roads lead to the sea* and *Dismemberment* (Auckland University Press), and two novels, *Reconnaissance* and *Love in the Land of Midas* (Penguin NZ).

In 2005 she moved to Edinburgh, Scotland, and wrote *Street Without a Name* (Granta, 2008), a coming-of-age story set in the twilight years of totalitarian Communism, shortlisted for the Prix Européen du Livre and the Stanford-Dolman Travel Book Awards. Her memoir-history, *Twelve Minutes of Love* (Granta, 2011), blends a tale of obsession and migration with a history of the Argentine tango, and was shortlisted for the Scottish Mortgage Investment Book Awards. *Villa Pacifica* (Alma Books, 2011), a novel with an Ecuadorian setting, came out at the same time.

Border: a journey to the edge of Europe (Granta/Graywolf, 2017) explores the remote triple borderlands of Bulgaria, Turkey and Greece where the easternmost stretch of the Iron Curtain ran. Described by the British Academy Prize jury as 'being about the essence of place and the essence of human encounter', its narratives weave into a panoramic study of how borderlines shape human destiny through time. *Border* won the British Academy's Al-Rodhan Prize for Global Cultural Understanding, the Saltire Scottish Book of the Year, the Edward Stanford-Dolman Travel Book of the Year, and the inaugural Highlands Book Prize. It was shortlisted for the Baillie-Gifford Prize, the Bread and Roses Prize, the Duff Cooper Prize, the Royal Society of Literature Ondaatje Prize, the National Book Critics Circle Awards (USA), and the Gordon Burn Prize.

Kapka Kassabova lives in the Highlands of Scotland. She was a juror for the Neustadt Prize (2019-2020), and was on the judging panel for the International Dublin Book Award (2017). Her most recent book is *To the Lake: a Balkan journey of war and peace* (Granta/Graywolf, 2020).

KAPKA KASSABOVA

GEOGRAPHY FOR THE LOST

BLOODAXE BOOKS

Copyright © Kapka Kassabova 2007

ISBN: 978 1 85224 765 2

First published 2007 by
Bloodaxe Books Ltd,
Eastburn,
South Park,
Hexham,
Northumberland NE46 1BS.

www.bloodaxebooks.com
For further information about Bloodaxe titles
please visit our website and join our mailing list
or write to the above address for a catalogue.

Supported using public funding by
ARTS COUNCIL
ENGLAND

Cover design: Neil Astley & Pamela Robertson-Pearce.

This is a digital reprint of the 2007 edition.

For Marti Friedlander,
photographer and person extraordinaire.
Born into loss, she made her own rich geographies.

ACKNOWLEDGEMENTS

Acknowledgements are due to the editors of the following publications where some of these poems have previously appeared: *Casa de Tiempo* (Mexico), *El Aleph* (Colombia), *Landfall* (New Zealand), New Zealand electronic poetry centre NZEPC, *Poetry London*, *Poetry Review*, *Street 45* at Galway Arts Centre, *The Times Literary Supplement* and *Writing on the Wall* (Arts UK, 2006). Two of the poems in the Berlin sequence first appeared in my collection *Someone else's life* (Bloodaxe Books, 2003).

I would like to thank David and Helen Constantine at *Modern Poetry in Translation* for commissioning the auto-biographical essay 'Skipping Over Invisible Borders' for the their issue 'Between the Languages'. This essay also appeared in *Landfall* (NZ).

I thank the Authors' Foundation at the Society of Authors (UK) for the grant which helped me complete this book.

Grateful acknowledgements to Creative New Zealand for a Berlin Writer's Residency in 2003 when some of these poems were written.

Many thanks to Steve Chettle in Newcastle for including me in his terrific project Writing on the Wall, which is how the *Roman Blues* sequence in this volume came to be written.

Heartfelt thanks to Enrique Moya in Vienna for taking it upon himself to translate and take some of these poems to South America.

Affectionate thanks to Clive James for his invaluable and generous literary friendship over the last four years.

CONTENTS

Geography for the Lost

The outlines of the hills are clear, very clear.
The stones are full of stately glee.
We don't know what has brought us here.
We don't know what will make us flee.

Seagulls in free fall, marbled weather –
with or without us, this city is complete,
and other cities for that matter,
and villages, and countrysides. They sleep

in peace without us. Yes, an insult. Never mind,
we're here. Uninvited, but we're here.
We even have a window, and we're pleased to find:
the outlines of the hills are clear, very clear.

We Are the Tenants

I consult my great itinerary of confusions
and it appears we've arrived
in the North. The seagulls glide,
inordinately large and slow,
over the vigilant stone, hungry for lost souls.
The hills are packed like cement,
the cemeteries lush with centuries of flesh.
The people smile with missing teeth
like hosts of a drunk party. Clearly,
the North has been here forever.

We have been nowhere forever.
We are the ones possessed by arrival.
We wake up with the cockroaches
of strange mornings. We smell the hopes,
the disappointments of months before.
Old mail piles up, their lives were temporary
just like ours. We have arrived in the North just
as we arrived in the South before, to sleep
above courtyards where immigrant children
call out to their future which is our present,

and the hills answer back with seagull cries,
and the chimneys of other times prop up the sky
like exclamation marks in sentences
that we must write in order to be real. Here,
here they are. But this is not enough.
We are the tenants of imaginary floors.
No matter how high the windows,
the ocean of the North remains invisible,
like the kingdom of some Pied Piper
who will sound, one day,
the horn of our departure.

I want to be a tourist

I imagine my life as a city
somewhere in the third world, or the second.
And I want to be a tourist
in the city of my life.

I want to stroll in shorts and baseball hat,
with laminated maps and dangling cameras.
I want to find things for the first time.
Look, they were put there just for me!

I want a room with musty curtains.
I want a view of rubbish dumps and urchins.
I want food poisoning, the dust of traffic
in the mouth, the thrill of others' misery.

Let me be a tourist in the city of my life.
Give me over-priced coffee in the square,
let me visit briefly the mausoleum of the past
and photograph its mummy,

give me the open sewers, the stunted dreams,
the jubilation of ruins, the lepers, the dogs,
give me signs in a funny language that I never
have to learn. Then take my money and let me go.

Our Names Long and Foreign

They squint in the September sun
of nineteen thirty-nine,
of nineteen forty-eight,
of nineteen sixty-two.
Here, one of them is born,
a piece of dark flesh in a dark time.
Classroom, ribbons in the hair.
Here, one of them goes across
the border to get married,
and be lonely and homesick,
and eat from despair.
Her brother gets divorced,
the second cousin's crowned
the town's beauty and has twins,
the other brother comes back from the war
and almost drowns
in the lake, then comes the other war,
or isn't that the war before?
Here, the twins without a mother.
The beautiful go first, and then the good.
And then the other way.
It's hard to say, the ink of years
is smudged by tears from nineteen thirty-nine.
Here, borders lift, the family meets
after seven years. Nervous smiles.
Their shadows stretch across the pier,
beach, veranda, cypress, pine.
The lake has no reflections,
the babies are anonymous,
the children mute as graves,
the adults in a slow decline.
They wave, they smile,
they're happy, but they feel
there's something on the other side
behind the camera
that's pitiless and wild.

No matter how much flesh
and hope they throw at it,
it gets them in the end,
they and their children who smile
in black and white, then colour.

Hello! they call out
from the shadow of September,
and trip into unmarked containers
stacked in silent rooms,
our names long and foreign
in the mouths of the unborn.

The Travel Guide to the Country of Your Birth

which

has over 300 natural lakes

is one of the oldest countries in Europe

has something for everyone, in every season

occupies the north-east part of the Balkan Peninsula

sits on the Black Sea to the East and the Danube to the North

offers white-sand beaches, mystic mountains, and ancient towns

has the Balkan range, which is part of the Alpine-Himalayan chain

has 378 kilometres of Black Sea coast. The Black Sea is closed and non-tidal, and has 90% anoxic water

has a moderate continental climate: winters (November to February) are cold and dry, temperatures reach -10

is the place where in dark, empty apartments the people you love live inside mirrors

The Argentine

1

I went dancing in Buenos Aires.
A man with a pony tail and German looks
came up to me and said:
'I'm from here. But everyone thinks I'm German.
Wherever I go, I can't be local. Can you believe it?
The tragedy of our nation.'
I'm sorry, I said.
'That's okay, he said, it's not your fault.'

The second night, he came up to me and said:
'I can see you're in love. Love is a terrible thing.
Can't eat, can't sleep, suffer like a dog.
Love is exile from the self, you know.
But I have good news for you: it will pass,
you'll be happy again. Trust me,
my wife is a psychologist.'
And you? – I asked.
'I'm a DJ. Unemployed. Can you believe it?
We live in Brazil.'

The third night, he wasn't there.
When his country finally collapsed,
he wrote from Brazil, saying:
'Argentina is in ruins
but I have my own show now,
where I play tango and people come to pretend
they are dancing, happy, and in love.
Can you believe it?
They are all Argentines of course.
And what have I become, you ask?
Pornographer of exile.'

2 *(a year later)*

Welcome to the club
of the broken-hearted, he wrote,
I too split from my wife. She agreed –
she's a psychologist.
You're angry too?
It's normal to be angry. I tell you what:
It could be worse. You could have lost your legs
as well. And there goes tango for you, adios.
Luckily, you have your legs. What do you mean, too sad to dance?
Don't make it harder on yourself, chica.

You're back in Auckland?
I'm back in Buenos Aires.
Here I can walk around
with my hangdog face and blend in,
no need to pretend
that I am dancing, happy, and in love.
No work for DJs here,
but I give lessons to the club-footed,
and take their money. Then I read the paper
and laugh. I walk everywhere, it saves
a hell of a lot of worthless pesos.
I walk and inspect the ruins.
I find comfort in ruins, don't you?
I like to sit down with a sandwich,
have a picnic, watch the dust settle
into fresh new ruins. And so on.
But let's not turn this into a history lesson.

When will you come to Buenos Aires?
So much misery
will cheer you up, you'll see.

Yours in exile from Brazil:
Carlos, DJ of the past.

Mister Hu

I often think of Mr Hu

He had a bar called *Mister Hu*.
Drunk, his wife got pregnant from an ex.
Drunk, he shrank into the night
to die of heartbreak. But he didn't.
He wrote short stories in the winter and lived them out
with small blonde women hungry for exotic thrills.
He loved it but he couldn't love them.
Looking at his thin legs in the bath,
he thought that surely, not everything was lost
although it felt that way.

I often think of Mister Hu
who didn't know the word for pun.
Wretched, laughing from behind cigars,
speaking every language with an accent,
he didn't give up. He went dancing.
He had dreams. Perhaps he was a little happy.
Looking at my thin legs in the bath,
I think that surely, there must be more
to Mr Hu's life, surely,
than gestures of longing and loss.

Dancing with Mr Hu

Mister Hu, there is no one like you
in the whole city. You are elegance itself
when you quote Camus and the Rolling Stones.
You know everyone, you dance
and your eyes shine
with hungry laughter.

In the snow, the dance hall is lit
and couples turn in slow motion.
It's a fairytale and you
are the delicate king
smoking a deliberate cigar
under the chandeliers.

But Mister Hu, when the dancing is done
and the lights go off,
you walk under the werewolf moon,
your discreet frame haloed by fear,
down the street where the heart is hungry
and the breath freezes from the long walk home.

I see your halo, and I promise,
I won't misunderstand you,
or the way you kiss my hand
each time and smile
before you say Goodnight,
thank you for the dance.

Mr Hu Drunk

You wanna dance with Chinese?
Yeah, I'm little bit drunk.
Thank you. Thank you very much.
Last tango in Berlin...

Tomorrow I go sauna, wanna come?
Yeah, naked sauna, mixed. I don't look at you.
Then Naked Lunch, at sushi bar call *Ishin*,
it's mean single heart. Make Chinese happy.

Have you had Chinese before?
You don't wanna try Chinese?
Chinese good and last longtime. Free for you.
I can get no satisfaction...

Can I fall in love?
No, as long as I have cigar.
Chinese don't fall in love with no one.
Nothing gonna change my world...

Have I told you're beautiful woman?
I tell you next time. You're not free?
I know you not free. I must pay price.
Please please please, please me...

You kick me out already? Only 12 o'clock.
At home, just tango music, cut my throat.
I sleep here, I don't touch you.
You are so good, Norwegian wood...

Okay, I go. Thank you. Thank you for everything.
Yes, I find my way home.
Fucking Chinese always find way home.
The long and winding road...

Saying Goodbye to Mr Hu

I went to the Sunday market with Mister Hu.
It was early spring. He wore a cashmere scarf.
Have you seen, he said, a Chinese in cashmere.

When the music played and the moon was sharp,
I danced with Mister Hu under the chandeliers.
That's enough, he said, I get Chinese obsession.

'I have no place, the Gypsy sang in Portuguese,
I have no homeland.' Mister Hu began a drinking session.
You don't like, he said, a drunk Chinese.

When summer came, I had to say goodbye
to Mister Hu. We walked by the river and fed the geese.
Have you seen, he said, a Chinese cry.

email from Mr Hu: no subject

I don't blame u if u don't write
I don't blame u if u don't call
I just put some music in phonemachine
to tell u I thinking of u. Right now
my coolrunning chicken
is on the way in curry-truck.
Yesterday I cook biological pig
I'm not sure pig is happy to be bio
Pig just wanna be pig.
Like chinese want to be loved.
This midday, I read Fernando Pessoa,
it always make calm wenn depress.
I want write roman
about fucking Berlin and how to be happy...
Maybe one day you correct my mistake...
I want learn how to cook good
Maybe one day I be you butler...

Ciao my friend, smile wide mouth
hu

Lying with the Ghosts of Berlin
(for Irit Stark)

A Woman in Berlin 60 Years Later

This is the Styx disguised as River Spree.
In Charon's riverboats we huddled, numb
with hope and disbelief, and fear,
waiting for a signal, any signal.
Destined for the underworld, we were.

Buildings of national pride
cast their shadows over us.
Blind statues stood like guards
to tomorrow's better world without us.
The signal came, disguised as friendly waves.

Nobody knows me, I'm disguised as a survivor,
invisible among more recent ruins,
swept-up leaves, and streets with names
of those born at the wrong end
of time. I kneel down and push

a pile of swept leaves off the bridge.
Let the river take them away.
These are the words I've kept for now,
disguised as epitaphs to something
disguised as a museum down the road

because there are no other words.

Berlin – Mitte

I live in a haunted house.
I have lost my hunger. I have lost my sleep.
When I sleep, my dreams are not mine.

My sense of time is unstable
and I wait for anonymous
midnight visits. I feel that all
that is to come is inevitable.

I have my suitcase close-by, but it's empty –
I know I'll be surprised. I'm ready
to leave my possessions behind.

I look for clues around the house.
But the walls are whitewashed.
The ceilings are too high.
The floor has been treated with the polish
of this new, confident century.

I sit by the narrow window
to remember those I never knew,
for there is no one to remember them.
No one remembers numbers on a plaque.

I fear they will come one night,
after sixty years of absence.
I will offer them the house of course, the bed,
the kitchen table, but I fear they will say
that what was taken from them
can never be given back.

Mitte is traditionally the Jewish neighbourhood of Berlin.

Someone else's life

It was a day of slow fever
and roses in the doorway, wrapped
in yesterday's news of death.

Snow fell like angels' feathers
from a dark new sky, softly announcing
that some things would never be the same.

I listened carefully to doubts and revisions
of someone else's life, safe in my room of tomorrow,
a passing witness to sorrow.

Then night came and I was quickly
drifting inside that life. I was leaving mine.
Snowflakes continued to fall.

The street was deserted and dim.
Shrapnel wounds blossomed in walls.
There was no proof of the current decade,

and I could not recall
the names of faces that I knew
the smell of places where I'd lived

and why I lay alone now
in a vast, empty room, so far
from the sun, so far.

Lying with the Ghosts of Berlin

Tonight is the longest night of the year.
We lie, patient with the seasons
in the glow of street-lamps,
beneath the outlines of things
that could be ours, some other time.

To the sound of snow falling,
we must sleep, again and again
like diving into the soft centre
of each life we might've had.

Yesterday was the shortest day
of the year – a wing that beat just once
then fell into the twilight of three o'clock.
The snow has settled. We can hear it breathe.

I say we but I see no one.
The neighbour upstairs has gone skiing.
The people across have turned off their light.
The rest of the street is a museum.
I lie on a marble slab, breathing.

Whoever else is here now
will be here tomorrow.
They are measuring the beats
of my remaining blood.
They quietly know something
I am afraid to ask.

The Ghost of Anna Seghers in Marseille

There was no escape except the port
for us, we were possessed by departure.
We hung around it for years. And then –
farewell Europe. Africa, goodbye.

A man, a woman and a child
stand with ice creams in the dying sun.
The century of transit's over.
Their feet are planted on the shore.

Oh, it can take an age to know
how finite continents can be,
how quick the future and how short the past.
Before we've found out exactly

what happened and what never will,
it's time. I have an old port,
everywhere to go and nowhere to arrive.
Here comes the last boat of the night.

It collects the souls of the dead
and ferries them in circles round the port.
Come to think of it, the souls of the living
did the same. Farewell Europe. Africa, goodbye.

Parts of Speech

(for Chris Abani)

There is a verb for when
the madness of a country
turns against you

There is an epitaph
for being fed to crocodiles
because they could

There is a sound for being
unable to forget, yet humming
small melodies of hope

I know someone who knows them
and translates them
for the world

When the world tires of listening
he wears them on his soul
tattoos against silence

Hanoi to Haddon: life and death of a stowaway

THE BROTHER
First sand, then fish, then sand again.
This was his life, going in circles,
tired, without hope, then he left
for the islands, drifted in and out of our lives like dust.
One day he called from Hungary,
tomato picking, he said. He sounded happy
but we never knew with him.
He called each time from France,
Spain, Holland, once he said
'I kill a hundred chickens every day'.

THE MOTHER
Ten years went by. He only called ten times.
He had no money to send. I said why
did you travel all that way to have a wretched life?
He said Mum, I am sick of living like a dog.
I want to come home, but I need some cash.
I'm off to London now. I dreamt
he called and said: I'm cold in London, and alone.

THE LORRY DRIVER
He tried so hard, he came
halfway across the world,
he tried so bloody hard.
And then as soon as he arrived
some bastard ran him over.
That bastard was me.

THE BROTHER
It was my fault. I told him I was ill.
Now mother has decided
to get a passport in Hanoi.
His ashes are in London,
and she's sold the house.

THE MOTHER
It's time to bring him home.
I dreamt he called and said:
I'm cold in London, and alone.

Theresa Goes Home

Savagery, like love, lives in the details.
Theresa walks along a dusty road,
carrying a water-jug. The baby kicks inside her.
She squints against the midday sun,
the heat moves. Twelve militia thugs arrive.
She doesn't die from it, not now.

Savagery, like love, lives in the mind.
Theresa goes home with an empty jug.
The baby has stopped moving.
Out in the setting sun with trembling hands
she digs out roots with human shapes,
and cries their names deep in the dark red soil.

Patriots of Gujarat

She has extinguished eyes. She folds
and unfolds her hands, then
pulls a photo from a plastic pouch.

Samira and Salma, she says,
engaged. University students.
Their fiancés gave me this.

Salma and Samira. I could do nothing.
I couldn't watch, how could I watch.
I had to watch. Why do I live now?

The men came with big knives,
laughing while they did it.
They were laughing.

I could do nothing. I couldn't watch.
I had to watch. I couldn't help them.
Why do I live now?

She puts the photo back into the pouch,
and smooths it carefully, a sheet
over a sleeping child.

Boy Falling through a Gap

Look: this is a world of wonder.
It takes a child to see it.

He spots the gap, and who can blame him,
he knows there's always there
on the other side of here.

Surprises everywhere, wondrous lies,
the gaps in the fence of time
so many that even love
can't save him, love least of all.
And he goes, safe,
without looking back.
His mother turns, and he is gone.

Out there, on the other side of here,
he waits for us to follow,
one by one, later, tomorrow,
slipping through the sudden gaps,
laughing, each of us,
surprise our last gift
to a world of horror.

Ship Advancing in the Fog

I don't know why
the sound of the horn was near,
and yet the ocean was not.
Fog obscures the visible
and purifies sound,
which is to say: when nothing
is clear, something anticipates it.

I stood outside the door
and listened to a cargo ship approach,
forge its way past sleeping houses
and muffled street-lights,
and I was strangely calm –

as in a dream where nothing
surprises you, not giant waves
advancing from a personal afar,
nor giant ships. You are too small to run,
you stand transfixed by imminent disaster,
waiting for it to be too late,
waiting to be delivered.

Earthquake in Hong Kong

In the city where people take turns
to sleep in a bed,
a man watered his flowers at dusk
on a roof piled with garbage and clouds.

Down in the street,
the shark-fin vendors washed
the evening of its fishy slime
and crouched for a smoke.

At midnight, you heard knocks
on the door of your sleep. You looked up
at a forest of blocks leaning down the hill
like the spikes of a dragon moving his tail.

The misty mountain, like all threats,
was invisible. And in the hour
of trembling earth you saw
this was the source of an old dream:

you stand at a window looking up
at a beehive of lives and fire escapes.
There is no place for you,
and you have nowhere else to go.

Suicide Honeymoon

They were nights of frost and moon-wreck.
Birds fell from the sky like chirping rats.
At dawn, crows circled the remains.

Who would have thought?
Here in the tropics, among magnolias
and fishnets, here in the honeymoon suite.

The first night he buried her in blankets
to keep the sudden chill away.
The second night she took a beach-walk.

He lay in the four-poster bed
with four carved heads,
all dreaming that she drowns, waiting.

How to Build Your Dream Garden

(Mandála, Ecuador)

Year one. At the end of a dusty road, find a malarial swamp.
Drain and fill with earth. Get sick. Curse the day you came.

Year two. Construct a wooden cabin with shells for doorknobs,
        mist for glass.
Lie and listen to the waves. Remember, you were sick *before* you came.

Year three. Plant seeds. The earth muffles the past with leaves
and roots. Now wait for someone to come and understand.

Year four. The coloured birds of paradise arrive, the iguanas balance
on the plants. Lost strangers come and never leave. Smile knowingly.

Year ten. Stop counting, isn't this why you came? Now dream to the beat
of waves the only dream that's left, dream that the garden goes to seed,

the iguanas grow to monsters and gore the strangers in the dust.
The locals talk for generations. And the sea, the sea takes care of
        everything.

Middle-aged Couple Watch a Pacific Sunset

(for my parents in Mission Bay)

A strange light came down tonight.
The ocean promenade
became a path.

The sea-rocks turned towards the moon
like silver-foil reflections
of worlds that could be ours

if only we believed in them.
And that was the problem:
believing is more than seeing.

We kept walking and watching
the miracle shrink behind the hills,
which is the way of all sunsets

but this one was different,
as if the last of something
would be gone.

Some stopped and watched,
while others were afraid
and kept their backs to it –

the man in shorts and pulled-up socks,
for instance, his legs the arch
where middle age slumps into old.

And suddenly, like him, we started sliding
from our best lives, here at the slippery
centre, and we ran

behind the moving sky
in a stupor of transience,
in a slow motion of terror.

God, we felt like yelling,
how much remains to us,
how do we measure it?

But we're inhibited and sceptical.
We just held hands.
Then it was gone behind the hill.

Dusk fell and we walked on.
This is the only world,
this is the only measure.

Postcard from Paradise

There's nothing like a tropical cyclone
to usher in the end of summer
in a scenic house with the perfect friends.
The situation is this:

the rivers have risen overnight,
the mountains become eclipsed.
The sea-birds flap like dirty laundry.
The bitter ocean saps the wine.

Besides, the islands have made
their tedious point about the virtues
of standing still, and the water is
no longer tempting and forever cold.

Moreover, the meat is eaten,
the book spines are broken,
the unrelenting happiness of couples
darkens the soul. In other words,

the unlived life beckons
from the other side of the cyclone
from the mainland reached by roads
cut off by floods. Yes, Help!
Love from all of us.

Another Ulysses and Penelope

When the seagulls bring no mail
I think of you in your confused domain,
seated on a crumbling throne,
with your tilted crown.

In Ithaca, I know, all languages
are foreign. All distances are great.
I comfort myself knowing
I'm your favourite memory.

And I'll finally die a happy death
when I sail into the light
of the oncoming day, past lands
celebrating new years without us.

I'll finally die a happy death
when I see your face turned by mistake
to another harbour, when I see your love attached
to your back like prosthetic wings,
casting a light shadow.

The Weather of Loss

First came the winter of the land:
snow in the head,
blood in the heart,
dark in the corners.
The sound of breathing alone
in the afternoon, for a long time.
The days ahead contained
a little of everything, enough
to believe there's another life.

Then came the summer of the sea,
white pollen on the new-laid roads.
You moved, and there was grime
and heat and even beauty
in the shimmer of the after-world.
Your shadow followed, slightly taller
than you and slightly stooped.
You had a little of everything, enough
to believe it's another life.

Steve's Last Summer

Once, we moved into the High Street
of an almost charming town,
in a top-floor flat above the Cake Shop,
next to the Salvation Army,
and across from Lloyds.

A homeless man called Steve
drew houses in coloured ink
and told tall tales about a life
he never had, and we believed him.
He died a year later – overdose.

That summer, bells announced the evening.
The whistle of pigeon and train began the day.
It was the present, but as in times
of great happiness or grief,
I thought of it in the past tense, like this:

I climbed the narrow stairs to the top.
When you stood up, you touched the ceiling.
The damp of centuries hummed in the corners.
Down on the steps of Lloyds, Steve chewed
his last year of hunger. Steve coloured in his houses.
Then slept inside a box.

One night you stood in the window,
at the end of a rope lifting a bed,
and the whole street watched:
the shop-owners, the late visitors in town,
the drunkards spilling out of pubs,
Steve with his dirty blanket.

They pushed up, held their breath,
and finally clapped in the dusk
when the bed made it and
you shook the sweat from your hair.

Goodnight, Steve shouted
and didn't move. Goodnight.

Everybody knew it was love,
he said the next day with a toothless grin.
Whenever they think of it,
they'll think of it in the past tense, he said,
like a story without an end, like this:

there was a top flat in the High Street
of an almost charming town,
there was a flying bed, a man
under the roof and a woman beside him,
there was a tramp below, or maybe not,
and it was summer.

Another Country

(for Martin and Heather Hillman)

I walk and the air vibrates
with the meeting of winter and spring.
I'm crossing invisible borders
on my way to some place, to some hour,
where I have to be happy alone.
I walk and wonder how it came to this,
that I should think of our love
as of another country.

I walk and I imagine how
in that country we're young
and without fear we stand
on a Cape at the end of the world,
watching the souls of the dead
jump into the water and cross
the invisible border
where two oceans meet.

Housewife Unhinged by Six O'Clock News

Six o'clock news, worst time of the day.
The newly dead are counted,
tomorrow's dead are on their way
already, as the neighbours fry up spicy rice.
I'm waiting, I'm a war-bride swilling gin with ice,
and you are out in traffic on your bike.
The days are shrinking, I'm dismayed
this is the only certainty we have.
We are surrounded, we are betrayed.
The past is an incurable sick flame
that hollows out our better selves,
drips wax on our dreams, and stains
the future, where our bottoms fall,
our parents die, and various new strains
of salmonella, superbugs and killer-flus befall
our friends and unborn children, all,
and the glaciers lined like sentinels
along the edges of the earth will thaw
in time to wash away the corpses. Bells
will toll until they crack. I see it: broken dolls,
unfinished dinners, sodden albums, rolls
of undeveloped film, rats in the water. Plague.
And if we are already dead, we'll die again,
frothing, covered in carbuncles, vague
memories of better times nibbling our brains...
What, seven o'clock already! I smell rice.
And hear sirens in the distance, sirens.
You're out in traffic, dodging trucks and ice,
or worse, much worse. And even if you sprint
up the stairs now, all smiles and helmet hair,
it'll be too late, it'll be no use.
You'll find a war-widow rocking in a chair,
blackening her face with bitter print
from tomorrow's six o'clock news.

The Visit

You pushed the door and it opened
in the quick house of seasons.

I'd willed you away from my mind
like a wild river in a far-off land.

I'd lived seven years without you
which now I shed like seven skins.

I would betray anyone, believe anything,
if that would make you stay.

I held on to your legs like columns in a vault,
you held me like a spilling jug.

Our raft floated from wall to wall
bound for a place we'd never reach.

And in a moment of inattention,
I caught sight of the door, ajar.

I saw us through the door,
a tangle of flesh and fear,

I saw something closing in on us
like dark water.

Love in the Dark Country

Tomorrow for twenty-four hours
I'll be in the same country as you.

The sky will be constantly shifting,
the morning will be green, a single morning
for my single bed. And in the night

as the dark country goes to sleep
a church bell will measure
the jet-lag of my heart.

I'll open my suitcase
and unfold my life like a blanket.
In the dark country I will lie

all night and wonder how this came to be:
the one light left in the world
is your window, somewhere in this land

of thin rain and expensive trains,
and instead of maps
I have an onward ticket.

Mantra for long distance lovers

When they are finally together, they'll find:
the limitations of actually *being there* are many.

She won't write about him and to him.
He won't toss and turn, conjuring her multiple embrace.
She won't practise chronic longing anymore.
They'll have nothing to look forward to.
And all because they'll be together.

So star-crossed lovers, wherever you are –
writing an email, boarding a plane,
driving home from the airport
alone with your tissues – breathe deeply,
avoid abrupt movements, and repeat after me:

the limitations of actually *being there* are many.

13 Haiku for My Lover as a Young Man

*

Hurry, I said,
there is not much time:
he laughed, so young.

*

When he lies down
walls fall away:
I see the sky

*

When he stands up
the seas are shallow:
he wades through and laughs

*

When he runs, the earth
stretches in pleasure
offering herself

*

The city his head
his body the wood:
this is my country

*

He sang and he played
before I heard him:
no one is perfect

*

He slept in places
that wounded him:
hard, brief, full of stars

*

I see him better
when I move away:
magnified by tears.

*

In this photograph
he is hanging down:
smiling through a glacier.

*

Here, jumping in a lake
outside the frame:
will he find it?

*

Here he looks at me
and I look back, struck:
the terror of love.

*

In this one we smile,
in fake black and white:
thrilled to have a past.

*

Sometimes he sleep-talks:
hurry, there is not
much time.

Happiness on the North Sea

We came to a town that looked
like an afterthought of its country,
wishing for different weather
and foreign passions, dressed up
and ready to go. We were charmed.

The storm came within hours,
besmirched our summer trousers
and ushered a return to the hotel.
In other words, we followed
the route of all new lovers:

the beach, the road, the bed, the suspension
of fear, the entanglement of days,
the blurry edges of things, the false safety,
the treacherous conclusion
of the beach, the road, the bed.

My heart was fast, your chest was warm.
Oh, we had earned this blue room.
We slept but in the corner of my eye
the waves rose with the same word
I couldn't hear, and tossed it at the pier

and its burnt-out twin along the beach,
like an unwanted preview
from a future or a past in which
we sleep in blue rooms, and the waves
rise slowly to tell us something
terrible, and this is the last thing we know.

I go my way and think how

After we say goodbye on the dirt road by the sea,
stepping over garbage to clutch and part, as if before a war,
and the young man on the roof
of your disintegrating bus with no brakes
grins delighted, as if saying: this is life, amiga,
you are not protected in your sturdy boots
and nor is he, I go my way and think how
destinations will undo us, eventually.
In fact, as strangers spit phlegm in the dust,
their baked-earth faces shiny in the grubby minutes before dark,
faces unlyrical and without sunsets like the Equator,
I think how it's happening already.

I go my way and confirm
that those who squat in the heat are sick and chew
the cud of their endless present which is remarkably
monotonous, their only distinction,
this is what it's come to,
and I am just as indistinct
in the blackness of buses, in the haze of towns.

I go my way spitting phlegm in the dust
and it's suddenly winter, chilly stars light up the snow
of the world's biggest volcanoes with longest names,
white trees glitter and vanish like memories
of someone's Christmas, and as the smelly type next seat
reaches out a taloned hand, finally making his move,
I think how destinations are illusory.

In fact, the only certainty
is this half-broken window
through which the snow drifts in like cake-dust
for the party of your absence, to celebrate the next
destination we've passed at least three times now,
which clearly we'll never reach,
because hell is circular, because destinations are the reason why

we clutch and part, and clutch and part again,
thus making sure we're alive, or mostly,
they are the reason for moving, or shall I say for returning,
which is what we wanted all along of course,
the only thing we wanted.

The Quick Life

(for Michael)

In the winter we went
travelling different ways.
One night, I slept
under red rugs in the Balkans
and felt our child inside me.
So there you are, I said to the child,
there you are. I turned to tell you
the sudden news, then woke up.
The next night, I gave birth to our child.
It was painless and clean, and lonely.
I looked down to see and it was spring,
pollen snowed over the Danube.
The following night, the child
was learning to read – so clever, our child, so clever.
I woke up. I was knee-deep in the Black Sea.
Summer was here. On the fourth night,
our child was leaving home. Goodbye,
I cried, Goodbye. It was autumn.
I woke up in the ruins of my home-town,
my hair was grey. My love, I scribbled on a postcard,
we had so little time for this. We had so little time.

A house we can never find

We couldn't wait
to leave their house,
to lie with lovers whose names
are forgotten now, to take risks
with our minds and bodies,
to live in countries
that never asked to have us,
or thanked us afterwards,
racing through the years with rage,
towards something that we
finally have one day,
and which is no more, no less
than the certainty of not
hearing their steps
creaking, measuring the floorboards
of a house we can never find.

Sleeping in the Alps

My father's breath is like a cave
of dripping stalactites and echo.

My mother sleeps and in her dreams
the worst is happening, again.

Mountains surround us and muffle
the edge of younger times, the names

of places where we've said goodbye
and once again, we'll say goodbye.

And carefully I lie in bed, listening
to the sound of distant snow.

Mother and Daughter, the Translation

She says You look thin. Are you happy? I can never tell,
which means I wish you were ten years old, or five, or three.

She says Let's sit in a café, you're not feeling well,
which means Let's spend more time together, you and me.

She says There is a nasty chill that comes in from the sea,
which means I miss you terribly, don't settle here.

I think I might stay childless, she says over bitter tea,
which means I can't take all this love, this grief, this fear.

Self-portrait of Anastassia in 12 random snaps

(i.m. my grandmother)

This is me at eighteen, teacher in my small home-town.
How I hate it, the provincial minds, the pressure to conform.

This is me, in 1944, with younger brother in an army uniform.
We're young and thin, our smiles are full of hope and teeth.

This is me at my last birthday party. Cancer wig. I can't eat.
Everyone has tinted spectacles, to hide. I look surprised.

This is me and teenage daughter with the sad eyes
of the only child. I smile to compensate, and all is well.

This is me, beside the Škoda, on the way to holiday.
I frown. I am fat and he annoys me, and it's hell.

This is me and him, beside a cypress tree.
He looks bored, but I smile. I love these summers by the sea.

This is me with sun-hat and a heavy tan.
I'm beautiful, I have a small, plump child, I have my man.

This is me and waterfall. I wash my hand.
My face is hidden and I could be anyone.

This is with the family. The borders opened up, at last.
Our kids hold hands. The adults don't discuss the past.

This is me at fifteen, dark and big-eyed like a movie star.
But we are refugees, that's all we are.

This is me along that road eroded by the sea.
Another twenty years, they say. That's far, that's very far.

Here, my blossom girls, and me.
Unsmiling, thinking better times will come.
But this is it. This is as good as it will ever be.

My grandfather falling with a blanket

It happens like this.
He stands at the window one morning
to dust off the blankets. It's winter,
the children are coming to visit.
It's time for his ten days of joy.

And yet he wasn't always
an old man rocking in a chair
peeling apples with a blunted knife
apprehending other worlds
by a window full of mountains.

He loved a woman who turned heads.
They lived as if they always would,
but the future was inscrutable.
He was an accountant,
sceptical about abundance.

And sure enough, here in a jar
lie two pebbles from the lake
of her town. They covered her eyes
when she died. How strange it was
to think of her sometimes,

her gold-capped smile,
her fur coat, her soups, her blind stare,
how she became someone else
at the end, a creature of pain.
And yet he never asked for much, no.

He had the children in a foreign country,
yesterday's photos, today's letter,
tomorrow's visit, he wrote lists, yet something
was missing. Everything was missing,
no point pretending.

It happens like this.
He stands at the window and waves
a blanket at the world which gave him
everything, then took it away
year by year, a negative balance.

How strange it is, how easy after all
to never see the mountains, the kids,
to never say goodbye again. Seven storeys down,
this is the only way now, with a blanket
to the hard, welcoming earth.

ROMAN BLUES

Roman Whore Blues

This is the end of the world. The rain is like a flood.
My lover's in that city thirsty for wine and blood.

They brought me across to sodden Britannia
We met here – he from Thrace, I from Mauretania.

In my dance trunks, with my callused feet,
I am the centurions' favourite meat.

Life here is brutish, cold and sad.
So he went to be famous in Rome, or dead.

Again, they'll throw him to lions and men.
And if he dies, I'll never laugh again.

And then I'll die too, and be buried with no stone.
Words and stones are for the rich alone.

On this bowl is our story, I'll bury it later:
VERECUNDA ACTRESS LUCIUS GLADIATOR.

The past and future of Aurelius Marcus

At Carvoran, the mile castle is gone,
and the stones. But the lichen remains
to prove that here stood a man
called Aurelius Marcus
turned to the north where nothing grew
but wind and enemies.
He took a leak.

The plague was in the south, far away.
His wife in bed, his children too.
The soldiers shivered under the moon,
played dice, felt homesick,
and were lucky not to know
the future. The past
is another story.

Somewhere in between,
Aurelius Marcus pays
a stone carver and spells
through tears and rain:
SHE WAS MY VERY PURE WIFE
WHO LIVED THIRTY-THREE YEARS
WITHOUT BLEMISH.

From Claudia Severa to Sulpicia Lepidina

Briga, 100 AD

CLAUDIA SEVERA TO HER LEPIDINA GREETINGS
JUST AS I HAD SPOKEN WITH YOU
AND PROMISED THAT I WOULD ASK BROCCHUS
AND THAT I WOULD COME TO YOU
I DID ASK HIM AND HE REPLIED
THAT IT IS ALWAYS WHOLEHEARTEDLY
PERMITTED TO ME TO COME TO YOU
WHATEVER WAY I CAN
THERE ARE CERTAIN INTIMATE MATTERS WHICH...
I long to discuss with you. I suspect
my Brocchus wants to send me off
so he can take up
with the Barbarian red-head
who hangs around the fort
her hair shamelessly loose.
She set her sights on Brocchus last September.
And I'm a fool for loving him so much.
And is your Cerialis faithful?
How is your little son?
I lost a child last month, it just bled out.
Life is either boring or painful, sister.
And if we're lucky, the future will make
verse of our letters, shopping lists and deaths.
Vindolanda will fall, another Caesar will rule,
our unborn children will die.
And yet we have to try. Meanwhile...
ON THE 11 OF SEPTEMBER, SISTER
FOR THE CELEBRATION OF MY BIRTHDAY
I GIVE YOU A WARM INVITATION
YOU WILL MAKE THE DAY MORE ENJOYABLE
BY YOUR PRESENCE
GREET YOUR CERIALIS
FAREWELL MY SISTER
MY DEAREST AND MOST LONGED-FOR SOUL.

Farewell I Wish That You Are Very Happy

I'm sitting on a river bench. The plaque reads:
he lived, laughed, loved, and left.

And after him, things still grew from the Wall –
trees, houses, weather, childish summers,

winter mornings quick with hope and frost
as if for the first time,

cobwebs of electricity hummed overhead, the river
and the sky moved in the same direction,

past Vindolanda where a man called Maior wrote
I'M WARMING THE BED AS I WRITE TO YOU

past this bench where I receive the letter
though it's not addressed to me, past all of us because

such destinations are not for us, only their ruins –
the lone children of our love and laughter. And that's it.

Barely I have the time to make a note of this.
Barely he had the time to write

FAREWELL I WISH THAT YOU ARE VERY HAPPY.

Skipping Over Invisible Borders

A second language is a double escape: it takes you out of yourself, but also back into yourself to places you didn't know existed. To translate is to travel this unpredictable landscape every now and again. But I don't translate, I live inside two different languages. This means being constantly on the move, skipping over invisible borders of identity and meaning.

I was born an escapist and a traveller, which is why I was gripped from the moment my Russian teacher wrote on the blackboard a funny-looking sentence in Cyrillic, then turned her bespectacled face to the class and said:

'Today, we are going to learn Russian.'

I was eight. The year was 1981, the place Sofia. Leonid Brezhnev, the last serious Soviet dictator, died soon after. My Russian teacher wept into her fringed shawl while we froze in neat rows in the school courtyard, listening to records of Soviet army songs for hours. By then, I understood the songs. I also understood that something was wrong with us, with these songs blaring out of megaphones, with the way we had to understand them. So, as an unconscious act of protest, I tried to be bad at Russian. I gave idiotic answers in class, infuriating the poor teacher who yelled that I was lazy and broke her ruler on my desk. Being a language idiot was unrewarding, and soon I discovered that it had no future anyway. One day I found myself entertaining my little sister with a slide-show of Russian fairytales. I had to translate as well as I could for her benefit. My mother came in at one point, and praised me for my translation. I was secretly chuffed. I kept up my slide-shows, ostensibly for my sister. I started looking up words in the Russian dictionary, and this is how I stopped wanting to be bad at Russian – being good at it was much more fun. Around that time, I started writing poetry in Bulgarian – about railway stations and going away. I also read *Evgeni Onegin* in a bilingual edition, and was transfixed by the miracle of sustained rhyming translation. Gradually, books became the centre of my world. I stopped showing my sister slide-shows because I was too busy reading. It was a way of forgetting what was wrong with us, and travelling to other worlds in the only possible way.

When it was time to choose a special secondary school, I applied for the English school. But my entrance exam results in maths weren't good enough, and I only just made it into the French school. The first day at the Lycée Français, our sophisticated teacher Madame Lambreva warned us in Bulgarian that from now on, only French was to be spoken. When we feebly protested that we didn't speak any yet, she said: 'That's exactly why' and continued in French for the rest of the day. We were petrified. It was too much for the girl sitting next to me – first she started sobbing quietly, then crapped herself. Her mother had to come and take her away.

We were given between eighty and one hundred and twenty new words per day. I went home and copied each word several dozen times, with the religious fervour of a convert. It didn't really matter what language I was learning – it was foreign, it wasn't Russian, and that was enough. French took me out of my familiar world, and that surely meant it would also take me out of all that was wrong with us. We sang songs like 'La Normandie' and 'La Marseillaise'. Their geography was a mystery – Normandy, Marseille, those were mythical places, like the Underworld. We had marathon dictations in class packed with impossible-to-spell words like *inouïes*, 'unheard of': negative, feminine, plural, umlaut, and diphthong. It was very important to get the spelling right. Our French teachers were Mme Musaud and Monsieur Neuilly, and I stared at them amazed how human and ordinary they looked, despite being unattainably French. Once, I drew the Eiffel Tower in a drawing class. Mme Musaud said 'That's a nice drawing. Have you been there?' I was mortified. Some of the kids' parents were diplomats and they had lived in countries like Algeria, Libya, or even France. But not me. When Monsieur Neuilly left, he gave me his address in France and I wretchedly copied it in my address book. He was as good as dead to me now. France was an idea, not a real place. Only its language was real, and I clung to it as to a secret money-belt.

By the end of the first year, I spoke fluent French and read Sartre and Camus. In my second year, I translated Baudelaire into Bulgarian while stuck in hospital with an autoimmune disease. There was no functioning toilet in my ward, and the incompetent nurses had burst every vein in my body, but I could discuss in French the phosphate resources of the Balkan region, molecules with triple valence, Hegel, and existentialism. Somehow, this was going to save me, get me out of there. I already knew, implicitly, that when you are a second-class nation, learning the language of first-class nations is the closest you can get to a ticket. The iron curtain was like the Styx. Poor as we were, perhaps we could pay our way with language units.

Soon, my class-mates started talking about studying medicine or law in France after school. Medicine and law scared me witless, but maybe that's what it took to get to France? Then, one day, the Berlin Wall fell. There was a coup in Bulgaria and the government was reshuffled. The world as we knew it collapsed magnificently, and anything was possible. I was sixteen.

My father went to Essex as a research fellow for two years. The family followed. I found myself at Colchester Sixth Form College with a late 80s East European hair-style, the usual torments of adolescence, and rudimentary English. You see, I never thought I might need English. I had been preparing for France all along. My English teacher, the poet Joe Sheerin, talked in class about *Waiting for Godot*. I had seen it three times, in Bulgarian. I knew the carrot dialogue by heart.

'It's a funny play, isn't it,' he tried to involve the class. They chewed gum and couldn't give a shit.

'It's not funny,' I ventured, blushing deeply, 'it's sad, very sad.' Some kids sniggered. Joe Sheerin turned to me with blue eyes full of wonder, and said:

'Thank you. You see, in English, funny has two meanings. It also means strange. It's a funny language, English.'

And he smiled with all the kindness I needed to rescue me from disappearing into the black hole of English. When I wrote my first essay, full of grammatical mistakes, inventive spelling and semantic horrors, Joe Sheerin asked me if I wrote poetry. He suggested I translate some poems and show them to him. I was speechless with gratitude, I still am. By the end of that year, I was almost ready to start writing in English. Then our UK visas expired and we had to go back to Sofia to wait for new ones. Four weeks, the Home Office said, six at the most.

The early 90s were a dark time in Bulgaria: poverty, unemployment, power cuts, water cuts, shortages, mass emigration, and disillusion. Six months later, there was still no news about the visas.

My mother was diagnosed with a tumour and had to have instant surgery. In the hospital, they had no sheets, only newspapers. I stopped eating, just in case. It was an act of protest – against what, I didn't quite know. My father went grey overnight. He sat in the kitchen at night, unshaven and alone in the dark when impromptu power cuts struck, and ate cheese pastries for hours. My little sister was re-learning to be Bulgarian after two years in English schools, and sensibly trying not to make a nuisance of herself – the family couldn't afford it. My English boyfriend came to visit in the darkest winter of our family, and heroically fought through blizzards to buy Christmas cards for England.

We waited ten interminable months for word from the Home Office. Bored and depressed, I enrolled in an intensive Spanish course. One more language couldn't hurt, besides I wanted to read *Don Quixote* in the original. For a month, I sat in a classroom and conjugated Spanish verbs in a sort of incantatory trance. *Yo me voy, tu te vas, el se va, nosotros nos vamos, nosotros nos vamos, nosotros nos vamos...* The world was out there, and I wanted to go and practice my languages. All I needed was a stamp in my passport.

The Home Office sent us three visas – minus mine. After all the waiting, I had turned 18, no longer a "dependent family member". But my parents could hardly leave me behind. Fortunately, they had organised a back-up option in New Zealand. We became New Zealand residents before we even arrived in Dunedin some months later, thin and pallid from stress and passport complications.

On our first supermarket trip, my father bought twenty-five cartons of juice – every available variety in the supermarket – and arranged them in neat rows in the kitchen with a madman's grin. No more shortages, no more dark kitchens. But supermarket thrills aside, Dunedin at the time struck me as Calvinist, provincial, and distinctly untropical. They worshipped someone called Robbie Burns who was apparently Scottish, and they had a strange way of speaking: instead of saying *pen*, they said *pin*; they said *bid* for *bed*, and *fush and chups* for *fish and chips*. It was Colchester all over again, except this time my boyfriend was far away, and worst of all – my English had lapsed. I made no difference between long and short vowels, so that when I said *shits*, I really meant *sheets*. Fortunately, Dunedinites were much nicer than the kids in Joe Sheerin's class. I wanted to study English literature but couldn't muster the confidence, so I enrolled with French, Russian, and linguistics – my comfort zone.

I was a published poet in Bulgaria by now, and still thought, dreamt and wrote in Bulgarian. But pretty soon it dawned on me that this move was permanent, that my life from now on was the life of a migrant in an English-speaking country at the end of the world. I had to stop writing in Bulgarian. France looked more out of reach than ever. I had to start writing in English, translating wasn't good enough anymore, in fact it was suspiciously like second-hand writing, and I was acutely sensitive to notions of second-hand and second-class. If someone else (Joseph Conrad) had done it at the age of 19, so could I. But I wanted it to happen overnight, I wanted to start writing in a literary tradition that I didn't know, with a fluency I didn't even have in speech yet. In my unseemly haste, I became stuck between two languages. In my writing, I had let go of Bulgarian, but I couldn't go anywhere in English. I became speechless.

I entered the transitional muteness of the immigrant. If you can't formulate complex thoughts and images in *some* language, you become emptied of complex thoughts and images. You stop being yourself and enter a state of non-being, of invisibility. I was used to writing in Bulgarian like living in a well-appointed family house: padding on soft carpets, muting the lights, glimpsing fantastical landscapes from the windows, conversing with the portraits of my ancestors on the walls, browsing the endless library. I was used to bringing the furniture of foreign languages into that house too – there was always room for more. But I had never tried writing in another language – a completely different business from speaking well or simply conveying meaning. Now that I tried, I found myself stranded in a mental no man's land, with no shelter in sight and no familiar landmarks. Who were my ancestors? Who were my contemporaries? All I knew of English literature were the novels of Jack London, Ray Bradbury, and Harriet Beecher Stowe, and some *Hamlet* – all in Bulgarian translation. Where did I begin? Whom did I ask? I was studying French literature, after all – Sartre and Camus, my old friends. But they couldn't help me now that I was in the thick of Being and Nothingness.

Instead of being yet another foreign language for me, English temporarily became my non-language. And because my sense of self had always come from my articulateness, I lost my very sense of selfhood. I underwent an identity meltdown. Of course at the time I blamed it on Dunedin. But while I was miserable in New Zealand, I also hated Bulgaria and resented Britain for what it had done to us. There was no place in the world where I wanted to be – because without language there is no perception, and without perception there is no self, and therefore no place for you in the world. In other words, I wanted to die.

I became a professional anorexic, scratched my wrists, wrote preposterous, hysterical poems in English, and thought about quick ways to die, since self-starvation was clearly going to take time. But my parents had wrestled the monster of bureaucracy and the spectre of ill fortune to bring us here, and were now saving every penny to educate us and give us nice bedrooms and twenty-five varieties of fruit juice. I couldn't. I was shamed by my sister who, once again, was trying not to make a nuisance of herself because she knew the family couldn't afford another troubled teenager. Then one day, in the swimming pool where I went to burn off the fat I didn't have, I met a psychiatrist. He knew a troubled soul when he saw one and told me where to look for him. He became my Kiwi Joe Sheerin: for a year, he gave me books to read, including Sylvia Plath's poetry and *The Bell Jar*. By the end of the year, I was recovering: not just because Sylvia Plath could write about the way I felt in my psycho-linguistic bell-jar, but because I had started actually reading English literature. I had been given entry into the literary culture into which I so desperately wanted to read and write myself, so that I could exist once again. I was also meeting local writers and like-minded students. New Zealand stopped being a wasteland for me around the time I found a tongue to be myself in. Or at least to be someone.

In the meantime, I travelled to Tahiti on a scholarship. There, I discovered that I was in fact French. The Tahitians laughed when I said I had never been to France – I had the accent of *métropole*, I was obviously French. This threw me. Yes, I had wanted to go to France, but I didn't want to be French. After all, I was writing in English now, and I had a Kiwi passport. What had France ever done for me except feed me with vain hopes of seeing the Eiffel Tower? But language has its own agenda. It is a giver and taker of identity on its own terms.

Even now, when I fully inhabit English, and couldn't write in any other language, I cannot control my inflection which is a collection of accents. My previous book of poetry, *Someone else's life*, was reviewed together with East European poets in translation. Yet when I met East European poets at the Dublin Writers' Festival the year Europe swelled up to the East, and tried to find common ground, I couldn't – we didn't share a language or even a culture. To them I was simply an English-language writer with a Slavic name. In Britain, for some reason people think I am French. When I meet travelling Kiwis, they are perplexed when I insist, with a touch of nervous shrillness, that I too am from New Zealand – I guess I never learnt to say *fush and chups*. The only language in which I can pass off as a local is Bulgarian. But when I tried writing in Bulgarian once, I found myself regressing to the level of my sixteen-year-old self, which is when I wrote my last poem in Bulgarian. When I finally went to France, I queued up with my two passports and accent-free French in the "other" queue, still somehow vaguely unclean. But it didn't matter. I didn't need France any more, I didn't need to carry my currency in a language belt.

All this happened in another, distant life. But the truth is, even now, after several books in English (and the occasional translation into Bulgarian), my yearning for the original language house persists. Not for the Bulgarian language itself perhaps, but for the comfort of that home. I have to accept that no matter how much I read, how many weird, rare English words I know, and how many books I write in English, I will never live in such comfort again. The loss of homely innocence is permanent. The leather-bound volumes of Wordsworth and Tennyson are borrowed, a kind of lifelong lease.

Walter Benjamin, on his travels to Marseille, said that childhood is the source of all sorrow. It is also the source of all other profound experience, which is why inhabiting the ancestral house of language begins with childhood, with first memories and first picture books, with learning nursery rhymes and songs, and absorbing the moods of language while you are still a semi-conscious sponge. You cannot learn nursery rhymes as an adult any more than you can learn memories, even though you can learn Shakespeare. But a writer's adventure with words starts not with Shakespeare, but with doggerel and lullabies, with slide-shows of fairytales, with

70

the deepest, pre-language memory of a certain smell of damp leaves. I can nicely render this memory into English, but it's an emotional travesty because the smell of those damp autumn leaves is in Bulgarian. This is why I could only ever be a tenant in the English-language house, albeit a happy tenant. This is also why my poetry bristles with metaphors of restlessness and the search for some kind of surrogate home to replace that lost original place of innocence. Of course, above and beyond the question of language and geographical displacement, the loss of the original "home" is something we must all experience, in one way or another.

Once, I found myself at a festival of Latin American poetry in Vienna, I'm not too sure why. I read my poems in Spanish translation, with the Argentine accent I'd acquired on my travels to Buenos Aires. An Austrian poet read my poems in German translation. The original English poems didn't get an airing. After the reading, an Austrian poet came up to chat in French. A Bulgarian expat introduced herself in Bulgarian. The Latin American community shouted in their various accents. An Argentine poet swore she had heard my poem at a festival in Colombia last year. I swore I'd never been to Colombia, but she didn't believe me. An American expat spoke English with an English expat. Splinters of Austrian German flew around us. For a moment, caught up in this Babylonian cacophony, tuning in and out of meanings, I couldn't remember which language was supposed to be mine. And yet, I wasn't confused. It was a happy moment of escape from the tyranny of a master language. For once, I didn't have to worry about being a local, a foreigner, or worse, a thing in between. I didn't have to worry about not remembering how to spell *inouïes* or how to say *fush and chups*, and betraying myself as a shivery tenant in a threadbare coat rather than a stately home-owner in soft slippers.

Perhaps this was my true place: on the noisy, multiple frontier of languages, a traveller passing through, free from the constraints of residence permits. In any case, it was a moment of polyphonic bliss, like listening to the chanting of Gregorian monks.

Notes on poems

The Ghost of Anna Seghers in Marseille: Anna Seghers is the author of the war-time classic on exile, *Transit*, set in Marseille.

Hanoi to Haddon: the life and death of a stowaway is based on a *Guardian* article about Ky Anh Duong, a Vietnamese stowaway who was accidentally crushed to death by a British lorry on 5 October 2005.

Theresa Goes Home was provoked by a reportage on Niger in the *Economist*.

Patriots of Gujarat refers to the 2002 massacres of Muslims in Gujarat, India.

In *Another Country*, Cape Reinga is the very top of New Zealand's north island, believed by the Maori to be the place from where the souls of the dead depart for the mythical homeland of Hawaiki. It is also where the Tasman Sea merges with the Pacific.

Roman Whore Blues. The inscription in this poem was found on a Roman pottery fragment in Leicester. The other three poems in the sequence are written around fragments of Roman letters or tombs found along Hadrian's Wall.

Letter from Claudia Severa to Sulpicia Lepidina. Claudia Severa and Sulpicia Lepidina, both officers' wives, had a correspondence around 100 AD while Lepidina lived at Vindolanda for four years. There are two known tablets which record their correspondence, both from Claudia Severa.